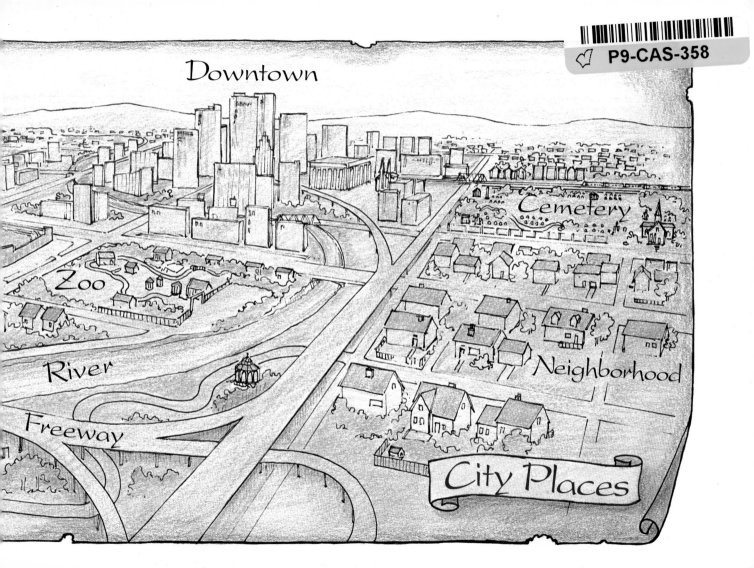

Downtown

Zoo

River

Freeway

Cemetery

Neighborhood

City Places

To Ann, whose enthusiasm for the natural
world inspires young and old alike—Dorothy

The Wild Wonders Series is supported in part by the Lloyd David and
Carlye Cannon Wattis Foundation.

The animals and plants illustrated in this book commonly occur in towns and cities
across North America. You may not see *all* these species, because cities vary in the
amount of habitat left within their boundaries. The selected species have been reviewed
and approved by scientists at the Denver Museum of Natural History.

We wish to thank Dr. Cheri Jones, Curator of Mammalogy, and Dr. Paula Cushing,
Curator of Entomology and Arachnology, at the Denver Museum of Natural History,
who checked this book for scientific accuracy.

Book design by Jill Soukup

Library of Congress Cataloging-in-Publication Data
Cooper, Ann (Ann C.)
    In the city / Ann Cooper ; illustrated by Dorothy Emerling.
        p.   cm. -- (Wild wonders series)
    Summary: Describes the ecosystems and daily lives of wild animals
that inhabit urban areas, including squirrels, mice, sparrows, and cats.
    ISBN 1-57098-298-8 (alk. paper)
    1. Urban animals Juvenile literature.   [1. Urban animals.]
I. Emerling, Dorothy, ill. II. Title. III. Series.
QL49.C6775 1999
591.75'6--DC21
                                            99-31231
                                            CIP

Published by the Denver Museum of Natural History Press
2001 Colorado Boulevard, Denver, Colorado 80205 www.dmns.org

in cooperation with The Court Wayne Press
Post Office Box 19726, Boulder, Colorado 80308
Tel. 1.877.929.6387 Fax 303.473.9303

in the
City

Ann Cooper

Illustrated by
Dorothy Emerling

Denver Museum of
Natural History Press
Denver, Colorado
The Court Wayne Press
Boulder, Colorado

Wild
wonders
series

Bright Lights, Big City

All day, cars, buses, and trucks rumble along the streets. Everyone is busy coming and going. Horns honk. Sirens wail. The streets are rarely empty of traffic and people. Trains clickety-clack along their tracks. Airplanes roar overhead. Even at night, under bright lights, the city never quite sleeps. It is *not* a quiet and peaceful place. Yet many animals choose to live here.

The city stands on land that once belonged to wildlife. As a city grows, some kinds of animals leave the area. They need large, natural wild spaces to find food and raise their families. City life does not suit them.

Other kinds of animals—more than you might expect—do fine in the city. They *adapt.* Some city animals scrounge human leftovers. Some make their homes on or in buildings or bridges. Many live in green spaces left among skyscraper canyons and miles of blacktop. A city offers thousands of small hideaways, from woodland parks and flowery backyards to weedy lots and city dumps. Animals live in all of them.

Although they are still wild creatures, many city animals are easy to watch. They have become used to people and are tame enough to spy upon! What do they eat? What spooks them? How do they act? Why? Read on to discover some of the answers.

Squirrel's Morning

Squirrel woke from his nap, uncurled, and stretched. He scratched his belly and twitched his tail. Then he scrambled down from his nest to find a snack. His buried nuts were mostly gone. Blue jays had finished the last of the winter's berries on the bushes along the river. But today, he did not need to scurry far over the grassy park in search of food. The spring sun was warm. At last, the buds were bursting on *his* tree. He nibbled hungrily, snipping the buds with his chisel teeth.

Rat-tat-tat. A woodpecker that was noisily hammering suddenly flew off. Squirrel stopped eating and sat up tall, his whiskers twitching. Below was a person with a dog. The dog leaped at the tree trunk, barking. *Chuck, chuck, chuck,* Squirrel chattered. He twitched his tail from side to side anxiously. His claws scrabbled at the bark as he fled up his tree. Barking and leaping made Squirrel nervous.

Squirrel sprang onto a power line that passed near his tree. He tightroped across it to reach a maple tree across the street. Safe from dogs, safe from traffic, Squirrel sprawled on a wide branch, his feet dangling, until he felt calm again.

Squirrel Snippets

Families

A female squirrel has two to four young in a litter (family) and may have two families a year. Baby squirrels are born naked and blind but with claws and whiskers.

Nifty Nests

Many city squirrels live in large, treetop nests made of leaves and things they find. One nest had a kid's sock woven into it! Nests are clean and cozy inside.

Squirrels prefer to nest in hollow trees. But tree dens are scarce in cities, because dead trees are rarely left standing.

Terrific Tail!

A squirrel uses its tail in all kinds of ways: for balance as it leaps and scampers, as a furry blanket on chilly nights, and as an umbrella or a sunshade.

A squirrel "talks" with its tail, too. Is its tail curved? Straight up? Streaming out behind? Is it twitching? Each shows a different feeling: calmness, curiosity, anger, or fear.

Buried Treasure

When nuts are plentiful, a squirrel gathers lots of them and buries perfect ones in the ground for later. The squirrel digs a small hole with its front paws, pops in the nuts, and pats the dirt down with its nose!

If the squirrel forgets to come back for the nuts, they are not wasted. They sprout into new trees.

Munchies

Squirrels eat berries, nuts, leaf buds, pinecones, and the sweet inner bark of trees. They also eat grubs, beetles, crickets, eggs, baby birds, and carrion (dead animals).

Enemies

Traffic is the biggest hazard to city squirrels. Hawks, owls, raccoons, cats, and dogs may also kill squirrels.

Fancy Footwork

Squirrels can climb down trees because their back legs twist around, letting their claws dig into bark like hooks.

High-wire Act

Getting from one green place to another is risky. Squirrels often travel along overhead wires.

Stoplight Sparrow

Sparrow found a perfect place for a nest, but he had no partner. *Chirrup, chirreep, chirrup,* he called, needing a mate. A flock of sparrows swirled down into the parking lot to feast on spilled popcorn. *Chirrup, chirreep, chirrup,* Sparrow called again, until a female landed by him and fluttered her wings. Sparrow fluttered his wings, too. Then he flew in and out of a nearby stoplight, as if to say "Come and see my perfect nest place."

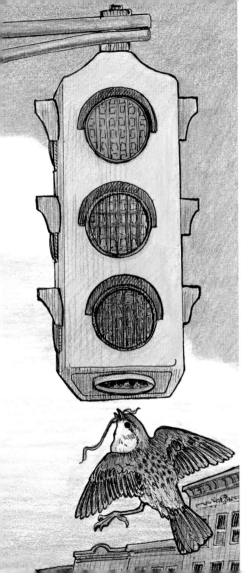

Sparrow had already collected some twigs for his nest. Now he and his mate found more twigs and bits of dried grass. They stuffed them in the stoplight. Then they lined the nest with feathers and bits of paper. About a week later, Sparrow's mate laid her first egg. She laid three more eggs over the next three mornings and then sat on them to keep them warm. Sparrow perched close by, ready to stay with the eggs when his mate took a break.

Twelve days later, Sparrow's four scrawny, featherless chicks pecked out of their shells. Soon they opened their mouths wide and wanted food. It seemed to Sparrow as if his stoplight family would never stop eating!

Sparrow Facts

Bath Time

Puddles are great tubs! Sparrows crouch in the water, flap their wings, and rinse their feathers to get rid of insect pests. Sparrows also take dust baths. They flutter in dust craters and get clean by coating their feathers with dirt!

Body Talk

A sparrow defends its dust crater from other sparrows by looking fierce. It raises its tail, sticks its wings out to the side to show their colors and size, and opens its beak wide.

Eggs

A house sparrow's three to five eggs are white or greenish white, often with dark speckles. After chicks hatch, the parents clear eggshells from the nest. You might find them on the ground below.

Beautiful Baby?

A just-hatched sparrow chick has red skin and no feathers. Its mouth is pink inside. Its yellow beak looks too wide for its wobbly head.

Immigrants

House sparrows (in the story) live near people in towns, cities, and farms. No house sparrows lived in North America 150 years ago. Then someone brought 100 of them from England and set them free in New York. The immigrant birds spread far and wide.

Food

Sparrows eat all kinds of weed and grass seeds, which they crack with their strong beaks. They scavenge crumbs and picnic leftovers, but human food is not very healthy for them. They catch insects in the air and even follow lawn mowers to catch stirred-up moths.

Enemies

Raccoons, cats, dogs, hawks, and owls prey on adult sparrows and their eggs and nestlings.

Canada Goose

The island was small, scarcely larger than Goose's nest—and safe. The water kept people and dogs away. Day and night for almost a month, Goose sat warming her eggs. She left only to find food. Her mate stayed near the nest. He honked loudly when other geese came close. Sometimes, he stretched his neck forward and rushed at the intruders to send them away.

One day, Goose stood up to rearrange her eggs. She heard faint sounds coming from them. A small star-shape appeared on one egg. Her chicks were hatching! At first the chicks were slimy, wobbly little bundles. Their downy feathers soon fluffed and dried. The nest seemed to overflow with yellow fuzz balls, peep-peeping noisily. Father Goose swam over to see what all the fuss was about.

Next morning, Goose slipped off her nest into the cool water. Her six fluffy chicks followed right behind. They bobbed like corks on the water, swimming in circles and paddling with their small webbed feet. Goose swam to a bay beneath a willow tree. The chicks bobbed behind, like a goose-train. Father Goose was the caboose, keeping his family safe from the rear.

More About Geese

Eggs

A goose usually lays five or six whitish eggs but may lay as many as eleven.

Let Me Out!

How do chicks get out of eggs? (No, they do not follow the eggs-it sign!) They use a special egg tooth—really a bump on their beak—to break through the shell.

No Teeth

Geese and other birds do not have teeth. They use their beaks to tear and crush food. Not having teeth helps keep birds light for flight.

Body Bowl

A female goose makes a saucer-shape in the dirt. She stands in this hollow and pulls nest stuff—plant stems, cattails, twigs, and grass—toward her. She shapes the nest to her body, then lines the nest with feathers.

Our Space

A male goose defends the space around his mate's nest while she is building the nest and sitting on her eggs. Once the goslings hatch, the male stops guarding the nest area because the family does not need it anymore.

Enemies

In the wild, coyotes, cougars, and bobcats prey on geese. In the city, there are fewer large predators. Adult geese are safer, but they may be caught by dogs or coyotes. Raccoons, skunks, snakes, and turtles may eat goose eggs or chicks.

Chow Time!

City geese graze in open grassy areas of airports, parks, and golf courses. They tear grass tufts with their strong beaks and clip grass as short as lawn mowers do. But grass *in* means poop *out.* An adult goose poops a pound a day. Watch your step!

Winter

Some geese migrate south in winter. They travel in large, V-shaped flocks. Birds take turns flying in front—the hardest job. Some geese stay put year-round. They have adapted to lawns, park ponds, and handouts.

Neighbors

A pond is a busy place, for most animals need water. Look for killdeer, mallard ducks, turtles, garter snakes, bullfrogs, dragonflies, and many other animals that live in wet, green places.

Mouse's Night Out

Mouse scurried out from her nest under the picnic shelter, twitched her whiskers, and sniffed the night air. The skinny moon cast long shadows across the weeds. Mouse darted to a shadowy patch and stopped to munch some grass seeds. Then she found treasure! It smelled nutty and sweet. It tasted crusty. Yum. Peanut butter and jelly leftovers.

Suddenly, Mouse heard a snuffling. She scooted under a trash can. The snuffling came again, and the trash can started to shake. Mouse rushed out and scampered under a bush to wait. An opossum clambered up the side of the trash can and disappeared headfirst. Mouse hurried back to the crust and took a quick nibble. But the opossum's loud banging made her nervous. She dashed toward home.

Whoosh! Mouse felt a rushing chill of something passing overhead. Just in time, she darted into her hole, her heart thumping. Her babies heard her coming and started to wiggle and squeak. They were hungry for milk. Mouse settled herself and let them nurse. Her dark, warm nest felt safe after the great outdoors.

More on Mice

Unwanted Guests

House mice adapt well to living with people but are not always welcome. Besides food, they chew up books, papers, cloth (for nests), and even electrical wires.

Many mice live indoors, in tucked-away places in basements or behind walls. Others live around airports, shops, factories, or warehouses—places they can find food.

Whiskers

A mouse uses its stiff whiskers to tell if it can fit through tight spaces.

Babies

The tiny pink babies are born naked, blind, and helpless. They grow fast. At ten days old they have fur. At two weeks, their eyes open. By six weeks, they can have babies of their own.

Teeth

Mice have gnawing front teeth and grinding back teeth.

Mouse Math

A mother mouse can have two to thirteen babies in a litter, although five to seven is more common. She may have five to ten (or more) litters a year. She *could* have a hundred babies in a single year!

Travel

A house mouse forages close to home. It needs a quick getaway from hungry predators.

Say Cheese

House mice eat almost anything: seeds, grain, cockroaches, flies, meat, leftovers, candles, and even soap and glue.

Owl

Did you wonder what almost caught Mouse in the story? It could have been a barn owl. Owls eat mice whole. They cannot digest the fur and bones and cough them up as furry pellets. Scientists study an owl's diet by checking bones in the pellets. They are mostly from voles, mice, and shrews.

Nightlife

Many animals besides mice and owls are out and about after dark. Cats, bats, skunks, foxes, and raccoons may all be out hunting while you are fast asleep.

The Waiting Game

Spider often had to mend her web after she caught large insects. This time, something huge had run by in the night. Her web was in tatters. It was time for a new silken trap. First, she spun a framework between two tall stems. She built strong spokes for her wheel-shaped web, adding a loose spiral of plain silk to hold the web's shape. Finally, she spun a long, sticky spiral, working in from the web's edge.

As she spun, she ate the unsticky first spiral. Her new trap was her lacy tablecloth. She rested in its silken center, waiting for dinner to arrive.

A praying mantis waited, too. It crouched in a flower, front feet held ready to snatch bugs or beetles. Watching, it turned its huge-eyed, pointy head slowly, trying not to be noticed. Nearby, a ladybug feasted on aphids. A garter snake slipped by, its forked tongue flicking. Everyone was hunting.

As the snake slithered through the weeds, swarms of grasshoppers jumped away, their wings rattling. One grasshopper landed in a tangle in Spider's web. Spider rushed over. She spread her spinnerets far apart. Rolling her prey over and over, she wrapped it in a wide silk shroud. Zap! She bit the prey with her fangs, injecting venom. Then she began to eat.

Spider Snippets

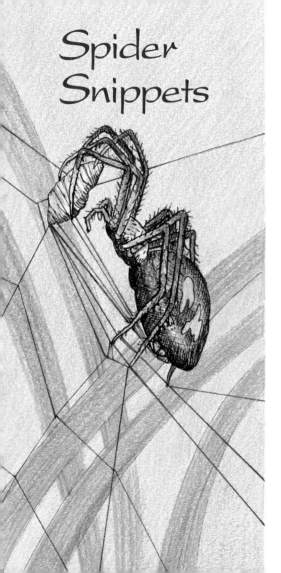

Silk

A spider makes liquid silk in its body. Droplets squeeze out from spinnerets on the spider's rear. As silk is pulled on, it becomes a very strong, thin thread. Spiders spin plain and sticky silk and know where it is safe to walk.

Wrap and Zap

Spiders silk-wrap prey and inject it with venom (poison) from fangs to subdue it. Next, they spit on the prey. The spit leaks inside and turns the prey mushy. Spiders slurp this liquid food, leaving bug-shells.

Spider Life

Not all spiders make webs. Some, like wolf spiders, are roving hunters. Others, like crab spiders, lurk in flowers, hidden by their blending colors.

Insect or Spider?

Do a parts count. Insects have six legs. Spiders have eight legs. Spiders have eight eyes, too.

Ladybugs

Ladybugs do not hide. They advertise! Their bright red and black colors are meant to be seen by predators. It is a way to remind predators not to eat these insects because they taste yucky.

Web Work

Web-spinning spiders do not decide what kind of web to build. Each kind of spider weaves its own kind by instinct. Orb weavers (in the story) make round, netty webs. Other spiders make web-funnels or messy tangles of silk.

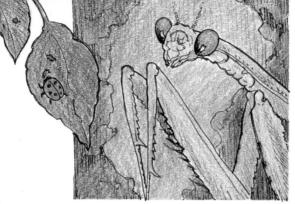

Pray or Prey?

A praying mantis gets its name from the way it holds its front feet near its chin. It might just as well be called a *preying* mantis, because it is a fierce hunter of insects.

Empty Lot?

No! Vacant lots are full of insects, spiders, and other crawly creatures.

Enemies

Many birds, including chickadees, eat spiders. Snakes, lizards, frogs, toads, and spider-hunting wasps prey on spiders. Spiders are even hunted by other spiders!

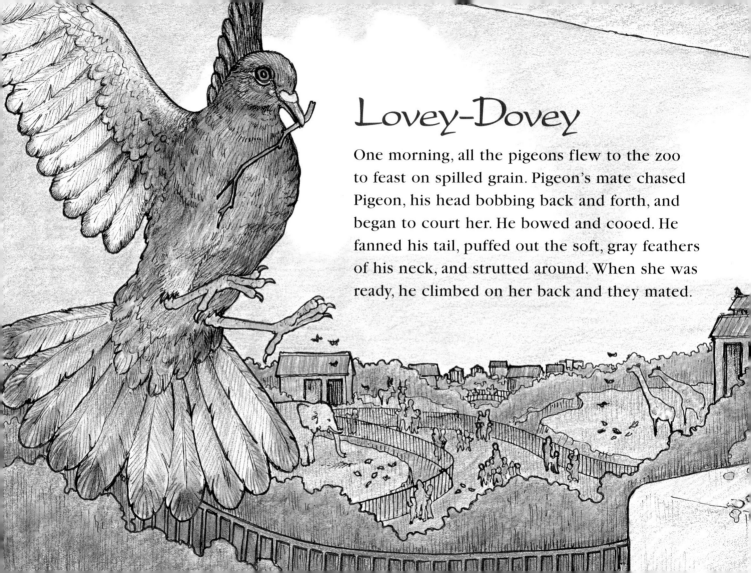

Lovey-Dovey

One morning, all the pigeons flew to the zoo to feast on spilled grain. Pigeon's mate chased Pigeon, his head bobbing back and forth, and began to court her. He bowed and cooed. He fanned his tail, puffed out the soft, gray feathers of his neck, and strutted around. When she was ready, he climbed on her back and they mated.

Pigeon already had an old, well-used nest. It sat on a ledge under a bridge next to the nests of pigeon neighbors. She had raised her spring chicks in it. Now the chicks were grown. It was time to fix up their home and raise a summer family. Her mate brought twigs one by one. Pigeon piled them on her messy, poopy old nest and shaped them. She laid an egg that evening and another the next morning.

For eighteen days Pigeon and her mate took turns sitting on the nest. Pigeon took the night shift while her mate roosted nearby. Her mate sat for much of the day while she flew to find food. At last, the chicks hatched. What a fine pair they were, with their tufty sprouts of yellowish white fuzz on their scrawny, near-naked bodies!

Pigeon Tidbits

Families

Pigeons mate for life. They have two chicks in a clutch (family) and up to five families a year. They even raise chicks in winter!

Pigeon's Milk

Both male and female pigeons make a kind of milk in a special throat pouch called a crop. "Crop milk" is a cheesy liquid, full of fat and protein. Pigeons feed this rich food to their babies. Crop milk is not like milk that baby mammals drink from their mothers.

Airmail

People used to have pigeons carry messages for them. They took tame pigeons with them when they traveled. To send mail, they fastened a tiny letter to a pigeon's leg and set the bird free. The bird would fly back home and someone there would get the message.

Sky Map?

Scientists are not sure how pigeons make their way home. The pigeons may steer by the sun, or by smell, or by sensing Earth's magnetic field, which is like having a built-in compass.

Tame Birds

Pigeons are also called rock doves, because the wild ones nest in cliffs. Long ago, people raised pigeons for food, just as they kept chickens or pigs. Some tame pigeons escaped. They were the ancestors of today's city pigeons.

Fine Feathers

Pigeons preen (smooth and clean) their feathers every day to keep them fit for flying. They take baths by fluffing and shaking their feathers in puddles or when it rains.

Baby pigeons, called squabs, are born with wispy yellowish down.

Enemies

The main predators of pigeons are humans, raccoons, opossums, screech owls, great horned owls, crows, and falcons—including peregrines.

Alley Cat

The truck beep-beeped as it backed up to empty the garbage cans. Cat gobbled down the last meaty scrap. Time to go home! She sprang lightly over a low wall, crossed a weedy yard, and slipped under the ramshackle porch. She purred as she greeted her kittens. They scrambled around her, nuzzling to get her milk. Cat let them nurse. When they were done, she licked them with her rough tongue, cleaning their silky fur. Then she began to groom herself.

Suddenly, the rotting porch over Cat's home began to shake. Heavy footsteps stomped. There were loud voices. A cloud of dust and bits of wood showered down onto the sleeping kittens. A machine started rumbling and Cat felt the ground shake. Home did not seem cozy or safe anymore. It was time to move on, and she knew a safer place.

Cat gently picked up a kitten by the scruff of its neck. She hurried through the weedy lot and down the alley. She scrambled over a pile of old planks, startling a cottontail. Then she squeezed through a loose board into a rickety shed where she sometimes went mouse hunting. It was dry and dark. Cat laid the kitten on a pile of carpet scraps and scurried away. With three more kittens to carry, she had no time to waste.

Cat Tales

Kittens

A kitten weighs two to four ounces at birth, no more than a small candy bar! Its ears are folded flat and its eyes are tightly closed. The kitten's ears stand up in about two weeks. Its eyes first open at around eight days old. All kittens start life with bright blue eyes. They get their true eye color later, at about three months old.

Kittens are ready to try walking at three weeks old. By four weeks, kittens start to play with one another and develop teeth.

Claws

A cat's claws are super-sharp tools for catching dinner and fighting off enemies. Cat prints show no claw marks. A walking cat retracts (pulls in) its claws so they do not get in the way or become worn. Look for cat tracks in mud or snow—or even in a concrete sidewalk where a cat stepped before the concrete set!

Back to Wild

Strays—cats with no owners to feed and care for them—go back to being half-wild. They hunt or scavenge food and live where they can. Any kittens they have are *feral,* or all-wild. They hunt for their living. There's no dish of fancy canned cat food for them!

Caterwauling

Yeeoww! Yeeoww!
The noises cats make at night can be scary. Two male cats may fight over territory (space). A male cat may yowl to find a mate.

Food

Feral cats catch birds, mice, rats, small snakes, and some insects. They also raid garbage cans for our leftover food.

Home Sweet Home

Pet kittens need *purr*fect homes. They should never be left to fend for themselves. Abandoned cats lead a hard life and do not live long.

Predator

Many predators, such as weasels, eagles, and bobcats, do not live and hunt in the city. But prey animals—squirrels, birds, and mice—cannot relax. They are still in danger from feral cats and stray dogs, who are the top predators here.

Sky Diver

Wi-chew, wi-chew, Peregrine screeched in his creaky voice. That *thing* was too close to his nest. He hurtled toward the window cleaner's platform and swooped within inches of the man's hard hat. Peregrine kept crying and swooping until the thing moved away. Then he circled swiftly and landed on the bare nest-ledge, next to his mate and chicks.

Peregrine's skyscraper canyon was so-o hot today. Heat drifted up in stifling waves from the streets below. There was not a puff of breeze. His chicks panted to keep cool. Earlier, they had feasted on a plump pigeon that Peregrine had caught. Now they were too full even to play tug-of-war with the leftovers. They were too hot to flap their wings and take little practice leaps into the air above the nest.

Far below, a flock of starlings flew out of a maple tree. The flock turned, moving as one. The sun gleamed on their black, shiny feathers. Peregrine watched them but did not move. Later, he would swoop into his canyon at breakneck speed and catch a meal—but not in this heat. Right now, it felt like time to take a quick nap.

About Peregrines

Feet and Beak

A peregrine dives down and snatches its prey in midair, using its strong talons (claws). It may hit so hard the prey dies instantly. Other times, it has to kill its prey with a beak-tweak to the back of the prey's neck. The peregrine carries its catch back to a perch to eat, tearing the meat with its curved beak.

Speed Freak

Peregrines dive at more than 150 miles an hour to catch prey. They are the fastest birds on earth.

Endangered

At one time peregrines were not doing well in the wild. Few survived to have families. Scientists wanted to help. They raised baby peregrines and kept them safe and well fed until they could be released in good nesting places. Some of those good places were on tall buildings in the middle of big cities.

On the Menu

Cities suit peregrines because there are plenty of small birds, such as pigeons and starlings, to eat. Peregrines also catch ducks, geese, rats, mice, and insects. Female peregrines are larger than males and can catch larger prey.

Families

A female peregrine usually lays three or four eggs. She and her mate take turns keeping the eggs warm, but she does the most sitting. After about a month, the chicks hatch. Both parents feed the chicks on the nest for the next five to six weeks. After that, the fledglings are finally ready to fly.

Adapting to Cities

Peregrines usually nest on cliff ledges, but city peregrines nest on tall buildings instead. They choose open ledges out of reach of people and animals. They do not build fancy nests. Any place on a gravel roof works fine, if it is high up and has a clear view of hunting grounds below.

Shadowy Hunter

Frost glistened on the railroad tracks and the stars shone brightly. Fox trotted from the thicket of brambles where he had been snoozing. He twitched his whiskers, sniffed the night air, then set off to find dinner. He scarcely slowed as he scrunched under the fence into the cemetery, leaving a scrap of rust-colored fur caught on the barbs. Among the weeds, he stopped. Listened. Was that a faint rustling? He pounced. Yum. Meadow mouse.

Hunting was good tonight. Fox gulped another mouse and another. *Burp!* He decided to save the next mouse. He scratched out a shallow hole and stuffed in the dead mouse. He buried it with dirt and leaves. Then he marked his stash with urine (pee) so he could find it again by smell tomorrow or the day after—and so other animals would leave his pantry alone.

A man walked by with a yappy dog. Fox slunk into the shadows until they passed, then trotted away through a tunnel under the freeway. Another fox had left its scent there. Fox marked over the scent with his urine, as if to say "This is my hunting ground." Then he slipped into a shadowy backyard. He fancied some birdseed and fallen apples for dessert.

Fox Facts

Eyes

In the dark, the pupils (the center part) of a fox's eyes are up-down slits, like a cat's eyes. Both foxes and cats can see to hunt in the dark. Both have mirror-eyes that shine when caught in a light beam.

Tracks

A fox cannot retract its claws, so its prints show pads *and* nail marks.

Red and Black

The fox in the story is a red fox, but in spite of their name, red foxes can also be black.

Fox Feast

In the wild, foxes eat rabbits, mice, voles, rats, birds, insects, and some fruits. In the city, they scavenge, too, eating bread, birdseed, vegetable and fruit peelings, leftover bones, eggshells, and even Chinese takeout.

My Space

The area in which a fox hunts is its territory. A fox uses its own well-worn trails night after night.

Double Meaning

Canines are sharp teeth used for tearing meat. Wolves, coyotes, foxes, and dogs—which all have these special, pointed teeth—are also known as canines.

Voice

Foxes have many calls: yaps, barks, yells, yowls, screeches, and churrs (rattling purrs). Each sound means something different in "fox."

Family Life

Newborn foxes are blind and helpless. At first, their mother stays with them all the time in their cozy, underground den. Her mate brings her food. Later, the female leaves at night to hunt and returns by day to feed her young.

Fox cubs first leave the den to play outdoors when they are about five weeks old.

Home

Much of the year foxes do not sleep in their dens. They sleep out in different places within their territory. When it is time for the young to be born, a female fox uses an underground hole left by another animal or digs her own den. In it, she makes a grassy bed for her young. She has many exits for safety.

Animals All Around

Even a busy city has hideaways that shelter countless creatures. Anywhere you go, there are more animals around than you see. Here are others you might meet in the city.

American Kestrels

These blue jay-size birds often hover above weedy freeway edges, hunting for voles, mice, insects, and small birds. American kestrels are falcons—birds of prey with long, angled, pointed wings. When they spot prey with their sharp eyes, they swoop down and catch it in their talons.

Cockroaches

These insects live in dark, damp places and scurry out at night to eat. Many people think of them as pests, but cockroaches are nature's recyclers.

Starlings

Starlings roost and fly in huge, often noisy flocks. They eat insects, seeds, fruit, and picnic scraps.

Norway Rats

These nocturnal rats use tunnels and sewers to get around. They eat scraps and kill small birds and mammals for food. Their rat-ancestors came from Asia to North America as stowaways on ships. Rats have more young than predators can eat, so rat numbers keep growing. Norway rats are city pests.

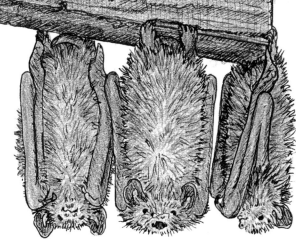

Big Brown Bats

These large, brown or copper-colored bats often live in colonies in buildings. They may roost in attics, under eaves, in chimneys, and in wall spaces. They eat beetles and other insects that they catch in the air—sometimes around city lights.

Did You Find?

Dog
Raccoon
Opossum
Weasel
Skunk
Crow
Woodpecker
Hawk
Killdeer
Starling
Chickadee
Snake
Snail
Dragonfly
Beetles
Bees
Moths
Butterflies
Elephant
Giraffe

Ancestors

Long ago, North America had no cities. Now there are thousands of cities. Animals live in all of them. But where did these animals come from?

▲ Some were *native* to North America but lived in wild places. Their offspring gradually adapted to city life.

▲ Some were *immigrants.* They were brought from other countries or came as stowaways on ships. They were wildly successful in city habitats.

▲ Some were *domestic* animals (living near humans) that escaped and became wild again.

▲ One, once an *endangered species,* was released in cities as part of the rescue effort to save it.

Tracks

Did you notice tracks or prints on some pages? They are life-size. Measure them with your hand to test the size of the animals' feet.

Treasure Maps

Front map: Find the cemetery where Fox hunted mice. Find the park where Squirrel lives.

Back map: Which animal lives in the neighborhood? Which animal uses the smallest space? Which animal visits the airport?

Animal Highways

Some animals must travel from one green space to another to find food or home sites. Do you remember how each animal traveled safely? Which animal . . .

• Crossed the street by high-wire?
• Went under the freeway by tunnel?
• Kept to the alleys?
• Went everywhere by air?

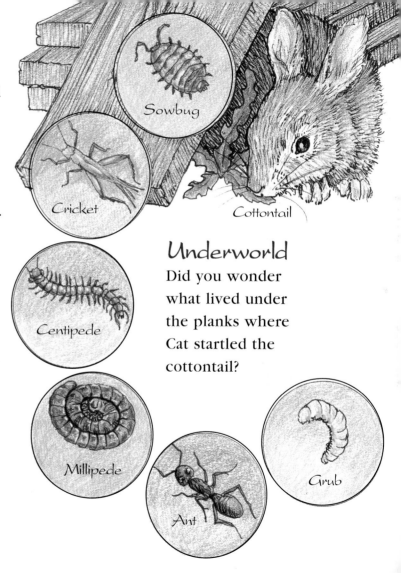

Sowbug

Cricket

Cottontail

Underworld

Did you wonder what lived under the planks where Cat startled the cottontail?

Centipede

Millipede

Ant

Grub

Links of Life

A city is not a natural habitat, but animals do not know that. They live where they can. They eat what they can find. Instead of wild forests or grasslands, they make do with airports, ball fields, school yards, parks, cemeteries, and other people places.

City creatures have never known wild, remote places. City life is what they know. They raise their families in vacant lots, under bridges, even on high-rise buildings. They spend their time finding food and trying not to become a meal for other hunting animals.

Would it be better for most animals to live in truly wild places? Yes. But the world is losing wild places and adding cities year by year. City animals make the best of it. They adapt to people. It is how they survive.

City people can adapt to animals, too! We can spare plenty of green space for them. We can leave green corridors, especially along rivers, so they can safely travel from one place to another. We can grow weedy yards with cover and food for the animals. And we can enjoy watching as the animals go about their daily lives.

After all, animals and people are neighbors, and we all play an important part in the way nature works.

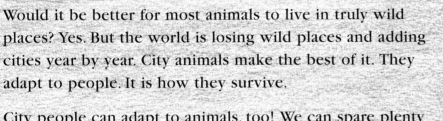

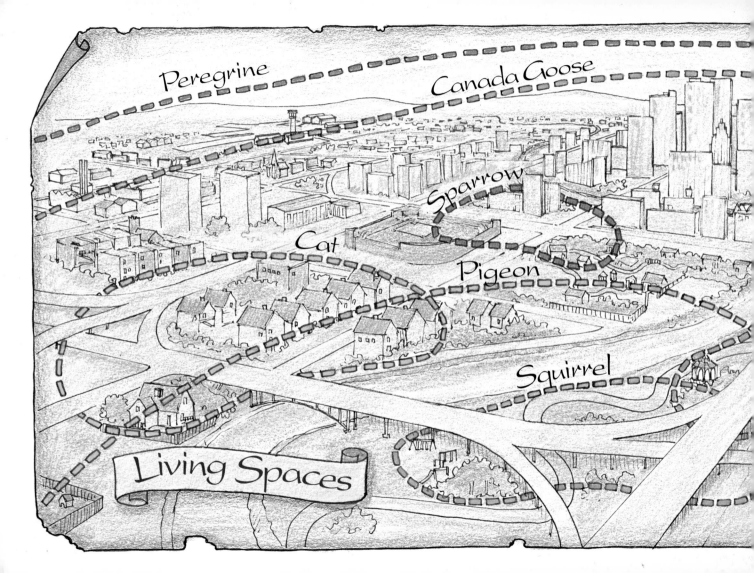